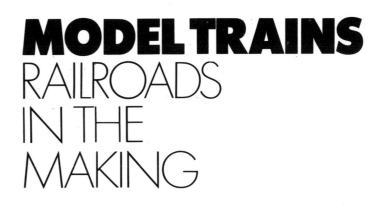

MODEL TRAINS
RAILROADS IN THE MAKING

With an introduction by Gerald Pollinger

ORBIS BOOKS
LONDON

Contents

All illustrations in this volume were photographed by Carlo Bevilacqua

Based on the Italian by Uberto Tosco

© Istituto Geografico De Agostini, Novara 1969
English text © Gerald Pollinger 1972
Printed in Italy by IGDA, Novara
SBN 0 85613 114 8

The world of model railways extends far beyond the confines of the toyshop window and children's playroom; it reaches into the homes of countless people, of every age and occupation, enthusiasts who devote much of their lives to recreating – albeit on a small scale – one of science's greatest achievements. Their enthusiasm is not misplaced: train modelling is neither a childish pursuit nor a mindless escape from the everyday world, but a hobby that calls for both resourcefulness and creativity.

This book, with its magnificent full-colour illustrations of some of the world's best proprietary models, is intended to provide further incentives for the dedicated train modeller, and at the same time show the as-yet uncommitted what high standards of craftsmanship are achieved in this absorbing field. The introductory text is addressed primarily to the novice: from a brief survey of the history of the industry, it passes to explanations of the technical details involved, notably choice of gauge, scale, power and trackwork, and then gives pointers to those seeking advice on the control and planning of a layout. At the same time, the more experienced model train enthusiasts will find an important comprehensive list of all the gauges and scales commonly in use, as well as a discussion of different types of equipment and loco classification.

The colour plates that follow not only provide examples of these classes, but also illustrate the variety of contributions made by different companies all over the world to the model industry, and in particular show the increasing accuracy and realism of its products. We hope that this book will draw new, talented recruits into the ranks of train modellers and demonstrate that here is a hobby that can fascinate and reward the enthusiast for a lifetime.

The growth of an industry

Models of railways and of trains are as old as the railways and trains themselves: a few fortunate collectors of the earliest models can point with pride to items that appeared in England in the 1830s, just ten years after the opening of the first stretch of the Stockton and Darlington line, whose first steam locomotive, 'Locomotion No. 1' took the rails on 27 September 1825.

Models of proposed locomotives and rolling stock had in fact been made before this date, and certainly a citizen of Prague, one von Gerstner, was using models for demonstration purposes as early as 1813. About this time also, British designers were visiting the United States of America with models of locomotives, while American engineers visiting Britain took home with them models of trains for the use of the early American railroad companies. Models such as these were, of course, fairly large, and the first miniature model trains as we know them today did not appear until about halfway through the nineteenth century. These were manufactured in England, in France, and in Germany, and were steam locomotives, principally made of brass. They were followed by tin locomotives made in America, and, at the end of the century, by wooden pull-along trains.

Prominent among the earliest manufacturers were two companies who still carry on the tradition: Märklin of Goppingen, Germany, and Lionel of New York, founded in 1859 and 1900 respectively. A number of other famous manufacturers came into the field in the early part of the twentieth century, including the British firm Meccano in 1915 (to become Hornby Trains in 1921), which had been preceded by Bassett-Lowke in 1892, and also Bing in Germany (from 1865 till 1933), and these were later joined by Fleischmann. In America the pioneers were Ives with Beggs, followed by Marx, American Flyer, and Auburn.

Most of the early miniature rails were of larger dimensions than they are today. During the first half of this century the most popular gauge (the distance between the two running rails), was $2\frac{7}{8}$ inches, although other gauges, notably $2\frac{1}{8}$ inches, $1\frac{3}{4}$ inches and later $1\frac{1}{4}$ inches, were also in use. The first very small trains suitable for table-top use were made in 1920 by Bing in Germany, with a gauge of only $\frac{5}{8}$ inches, and a year later these were introduced into England by the late W. J. Bassett-Lowke. Hornby and Lionel did not start manufacturing these little models until 1938, and in the meanwhile Trix and Fleischmann had produced quite a number of such models in Germany. (An even smaller practical gauge of 0.471 inches was introduced by the American company Harold Products about 1960, and this did become popular in Britain, although it has recently been superseded by a much smaller gauge, for which the track and models were originally zinc alloy toys.)

In order to obtain a certain amount of order and co-operation between manufacturers of model railway equipment, certain organizations have been formed which lay down recommended standards. These include the National Model Railroad Association of America, the British Railway Modelling Standards Bureau, and the Normes Européennes Modelfer (NEM) in Europe. Unfortunately these organizations have not always had all the support that they deserve, with a result that there remains – particularly in Britain – a confusion in standards that serves only to make the life of the modeller who wishes to work to scale standards somewhat difficult.

Model railroads and toy trains are two quite separate things, and the day is rapidly approaching when, as a result of both important new manufacturing processes and higher standards, the toy train of yesterday will become the miniature scale model of tomorrow, reproducing every feature of the prototype in exact detail.

The illustrations that appear in this book are primarily of Italian and German models, for the book originally appeared in Italy. In nearly every case they show a high standard of accuracy and attention to detail, for the European model railway manufacturers whose work is photographed in these pages have long made realism their aim, and their craft is shown pictorially to great effect. Indeed, when one can purchase ready-to-run models, or

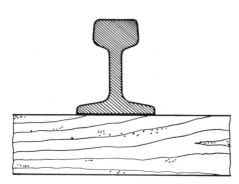

All model rail is allocated code numbers, which refer to the basic dimensions of the rail. The most important of these are the overall height, the width of the base, and the width and depth of the head. This drawing shows flat bottom rail in profile.

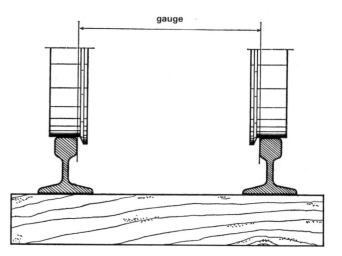

A diagram of the train wheels, as they sit on the rail. The width of the tread on the rail, the overall width of the tire, the depth and width of the flange, and the back-to-back measurement are all important for easy running and interchange.

construction kits of models like these, there seems little point in buying a 'toy train', and having second best.

Gauge and scale

To a novice modeller, two of the most confusing terms are *gauge* and *scale*, and this confusion is enhanced by the fact that these words are often used incorrectly – not least by some manufacturers, who are often guilty, for example, of indicating that HO and OO gauges are the same thing – which is in fact not the case, for each uses a different scale.

Quite simply, the gauge is the distance between the two running rails. In prototype railways this is generally expressed in feet and inches or metres, and in model railways in inches and fractions (particularly with the larger gauges), or in millimetres.

The majority of the world's railways use the Standard Gauge of 4 feet 8½ inches, and this is the one on which most model railways are based. However, there are many other gauges in use in many countries, and these have also been made use of by the modellers. These include the metre gauge (3 feet 3⅜ inches), used in Brazil and Burma, and those of 5 feet 6 inches in India and Argentina, 5 feet 0 inches in Russia, 3 feet 0 inches in Colombia, and 1 foot 11⅝ inches in Peru.

But whatever gauge is used for a model, it is related to the scale, which quite simply substitutes one unit of measurement for one unit of measurement on the original. Thus, on a prototype one foot equals one foot, and if a half-scale model were made of this prototype, six inches on the model would equal one foot on the original. Gauges and scales have been awarded symbols: for example, in the most widely used, the HO gauge, the distance between the running rails is 16.5 millimetres, representing 4 feet 8½ inches, reduced in proportion to the scale of the rolling stock used upon it, to a scale of 3.5 millimetres to the foot. The table on pages 7 and 8 gives a similar detailed survey of the other gauges and scales to be found in use in model railways all over the world at the

present time, tabulated in descending order of size.

Most of the models in the illustrations in this book are for HO gauge, with a scale of 3.5 millimetres to the foot, but there are also some British models included that run on the same gauge of 16.5 millimetres, but are built to the oversize scale of 4 millimetres to the foot.

In addition to these models, there are also models of trains for narrow gauges, that is, less than the standard gauge of 4 feet 8½ inches. Normally one does not model the larger gauges of 3 feet 6 inches and one metre that are in prototype use all over the world, but there are many models of the 3 feet, 2 feet 6 inches, 2 feet 3 inches and 2 feet gauges. The table on page 9 summarizes the most common narrow gauges in use.

With the introduction of the Z gauge of 6.5 millimetres, it will be possible to model narrow gauges in other scales, using 4 millimetre scale models to represent the 18 inch gauge prototype that is often used for public miniature railways, using a scale of 4¾ inches to the foot.

Power and trackwork

This book deals principally with model trains that run on a track gauge of 16.5 millimetres and are built to a scale of either 3.5 or 4 millimetres to the foot. We will ignore two of the forms of propulsion, steam (although it has been used) and the hand (which is always in use!), and concentrate solely on trains powered by clockwork or electric current.

Bing Brothers of Nuremberg were one of the earliest producers of OO gauge trains, between the years 1924 and 1926. The most common locomotive was a 2–4–0T tank engine, powered by clockwork or by a 4–6 volt accumulator (as liquid batteries were then known). The track was metal based with two rails for clockwork trains, and included a third insulated central rail for electric trains.

In England, Bassett-Lowke of Northampton had produced much the same trains as Bing before the Depression of 1926, and in 1935 introduced the Trix-Twin

Gauges and scales

NAME	GAUGE	DESCRIPTION
3	2½ ins (63.50 mm)	In 1902 the first commercial models appeared with this gauge. Three scales are used: ½ in, $\frac{17}{32}$ in, or 14 mm to the foot
STANDARD	2⅛ ins (53.97 mm)	Much in vogue before 1938, this American gauge used a scale of ⅜ in to the foot, or sometimes $\frac{7}{16}$ in.
2	2 ins (50.97 mm)	Not much used. The scale used was normally $\frac{7}{16}$ in to the foot, and the scale ratio was 1:26 or 1:27.
1F	45 mm	A fine scale version of a gauge ideal for use in garden railways. The scale is 10 mm to the foot. The ratio is 1:30.5.
1	1¾ ins (44.45 mm)	Britain uses a scale of 10 mm to the foot; Germany and the USA have a scale of ⅜ ins and a scale ratio of 1:32.
O_{17}	1¼ ins (31.75 mm)	Using English instead of metric measurements, this rarely used gauge uses a scale of $\frac{17}{64}$ ins to the foot.
O	32 mm	Appearing before the First World War, the British O Gauge is still popular. The scale is 7 mm to the foot.
OF	32 mm	Also with a scale of 7 mm to the foot, this gauge uses much finer measurements; the rail height, for example, is only half that of O. Ratio: 1:43.5.
O	1¼ ins	In America a scale of ¼ in to the foot is normal, and a ratio of 1:48, as opposed to the 1:45.2 ratio of O_{17}.
O	1⅛ ins	A number of Continental models have appeared using this gauge, built to a scale of 2 cm to 1 metre.
Q	1$\frac{3}{16}$ ins	Also referred to as a gauge of 1.188 in, this American gauge uses a scale of ¼ in to the foot. It has been replaced by O.

NAME	GAUGE	DESCRIPTION
HI	⅞ ins	Literally half of Gauge 1, this gauge was superseded by S Gauge. It has a scale of $\frac{3}{15}$ ins to the foot.
S	⅞ ins	Quite common in the USA, with a scale of $\frac{3}{16}$ ins to the foot and a ratio of 1:64; Europe prefers to express the gauge as 22.2 mm and the ratio as 1:65.
OO	¾ ins (19 mm)	Much confusion derives from the use by America of a 19 mm gauge with a scale of 4 mm to the foot and a ratio of 1:76.2.
EEM	18.83 mm	Originally called EMF Gauge, this was a British fine scale attempt, superseded by the Protofour group, using a scale of 4 mm/1 ft and a 1:76.2 ratio.
EM	18 mm	Since the gauge/scale relationship of the British OO Gauge is inaccurate, quite a number of modellers use 18 mm as a gauge with a 4 mm scale.
OO	16.5 mm	The most common British gauge, with a scale of 4 mm to the foot (giving a top-heavy overscale appearance but useful for including large motors in small locos).
HO	16.5 mm	The most widely used gauge. The scale is normally 3.5 mm to the foot and the ratio 1:87.1. Some models have used a 3.8 mm scale.
OOE	16.5	There are still a number of French and German models using this gauge with a scale of 1 cm to the metre, and a scale ratio of 1:91.
HOE	16 mm	Rarely used, this gauge was replaced by HO Gauge. It had a scale of 3.5 mm to the foot.
E	$\frac{19}{32}$ ins	Another rare gauge, also replaced by HO gauge with a scale of ⅛ in to the foot. The gauge is also called 15 mm.

NAME	GAUGE	DESCRIPTION	NAME	GAUGE	DESCRIPTION
QO	0.6 ins	This is a very rare American gauge, in which the models are built to a scale of $\frac{1}{8}$ in to the foot.			gauge. The scale is 2 mm to the foot and there is an active Scale Association. Ratio: 1:152.4.
OOC	14.3 mm	This Continental scale aims to obtain a perfect scale ratio of 1:100 with a scale of 1 cm to 1 metre.	N	9 mm	The British modeller uses a scale of 2.06 mm to the foot, which is a ratio of 1:148, and gives a slightly overscale effect.
TM	13.5 mm	A British fine scale/gauge ratio of TT Gauge, using the standard British scale of 3 mm to the foot.	N	9 mm	On the Continent of Europe, the ratio used to be 1:150, but in 1960 was standardized at 1:160, with a scale of 1.9 mm to the foot.
TT–3	12 mm	The commonly used British table-top gauge with a scale of 3 mm to the foot, giving an oversized effect. The ratio is 1:101.6.	K	8 mm	Only in Europe are there models to this small gauge, with a scale of 1.75 mm to the foot and a ratio of 1:180.
TT	12 mm	The original table-top gauge of 0.471 in, with a scale of 2.5 mm (European) or $\frac{1}{10}$ in (USA) to the foot, and a ratio of 1:120.	QOO	7.62 mm	Rarely used, except for special purposes at exhibitions, this is an American gauge with a scale of 1.75 mm to the foot.
TT–X	12 mm	A few British modellers decided to scale down the British TT–3 Gauge, and use a scale of $\frac{1}{9}$ in to the foot.	Z	6.5 mm	Introduced in Germany in 1972, this minute gauge is likely to be the smallest commercially. The ratio is 1:220 and the scale 1.51 mm to the foot.
HOO	10 mm	Known as *centimetrico*, or micro-gauge. It is in use in Sweden, with a scale of 2 mm to the foot and a ratio of 1:144.	X	$\frac{3}{16}$ ins (4.5 mm)	In 1935 Mr Reg Walkley produced a scale model of an 0–4–0T tank locomotive to a scale of 1 mm to the foot. It operated perfectly.
OOO	9.5 mm	Fifty years ago the first models appeared for this			

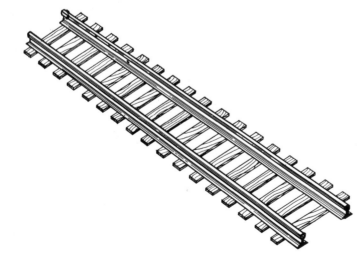

A level straight track is the only condition for the unhampered passage of wheels with flanges built to run on the same gauge. Complications start at curves, or where one rail crosses another, and to avoid derailments at such points the measurements of the trackwork must fit exactly those of the wheels of the model.

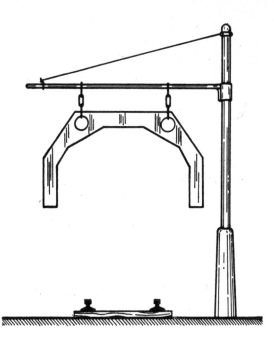

A loading gauge. This sets the limit on the height of a train so that it is able to pass safely under bridges and tunnels.

Narrow gauges

NAME	GAUGE	DESCRIPTION	NAME	GAUGE	DESCRIPTION
Gm	45 mm	LBM are huge German models. Using Gauge 1 track, the scale is 22.5 mm to the foot.	TT3n	12 mm	One British manufacturer makes models of Welsh narrow gauge railway locomotives and cars to a scale of $5\frac{1}{2}$ mm to the foot.
On	32 mm	Rolling stock for $2\frac{7}{8}$ ins Gauge, Gauge 3 and Gauge 1 use scales of 16 mm, 14 mm, and 10 mm to the foot representing 2 ft, 2 ft 3 ins and 3 ft prototypes.	OOn3	12 mm	To represent a 3 ft gauge prototype, one British manufacturer issues Isle of Man models to a scale of 4 mm to the foot.
On3	19 mm	One of the three standard American narrow gauge models, with a scale of $\frac{1}{4}$ inch to the foot and a ratio of 1:48.	TTn	12 mm	An East German company markets a number of models of German and Austrian equipment to a scale of 3.5 mm to the foot.
On2½	16.5 mm	The scale used is $\frac{1}{4}$ in to the foot, and this enables HO items to be used to represent both 2 ft 3 ins and 2 ft 6 ins prototypes.	HOn3	10.5 mm	On 0.413 inch gauge, many Americans model to a scale of 3.5 mm and a ratio of 1:87.1 to represent 3 ft gauge prototypes.
OOn	16.5 mm	Using 7 mm scale models – that is, those normally built for Gauge O – on trackwork half the size will represent 2 ft 3 ins and 2 ft 6 ins prototypes.	OO9	9 mm	Strictly speaking, this is OOn2.25 Gauge, using a scale of 4 mm to the foot to represent 2 ft 3 in prototypes.
On2	$\frac{1}{2}$ in	The second standard American narrow gauge uses $\frac{1}{4}$ inch scale models, and has a ratio of 1:48.	HOn2½	9 mm	The smallest scale for narrow gauges in common use is 3.5 mm to the foot to represent 2 ft 6 in prototypes. It is also called HOn9.

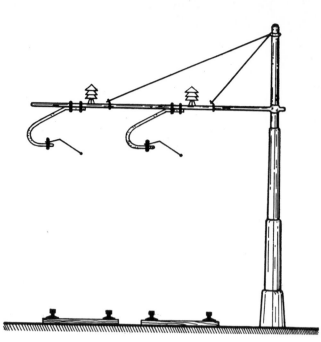

Right: A type of equipment for overhead pickup. There are suggested standards for overhead electric and traction power pickup, including not only the thickness of the wire rod, and its height above the head of the rail, but also by how much the wire can be offset from the centre of the track below.

range. Like Bing, this used a 16 millimetre gauge (described as OO), and the scale chosen by Henry Greenly of 4 millimetres to the foot gave a ratio of 1:80. The 'universal' motors operated on 12 volts DC (using an easy multiple of the 2 volts direct current accumulator – an interesting historical event in view of the future) or preferably 14 volts AC. Alternating current was used to reverse the motors, and later to operate remote uncoupling devices in the tender. The controller gave a continuous sequence of ahead, stop, reverse, stop, which was often unsatisfactory. The trackwork had a Bakelite base, $\frac{3}{8}$ inches high, with three running rails, each insulated from the base. This last feature gave the operator the unique possibility of having two engines working independently on one section of track: one loco had pick-up brushes for the current over the left-hand rail, the other had them on the right-hand rail, and both used the centre rail as a common return. Meanwhile, in Nuremberg, Trix Express continued its own separate development using a smaller scale of 3.5 millimetres.

In 1937, Hornby-Dublo produced its OO gauge trains in clockwork and electric versions, standardizing on 12 volts DC for operation. The products from the Liverpool factory were far in advance of anything that had so far appeared, and set the pattern for future scale developments: the trackwork was two-rail for clockwork, or three-rail for electric operation, the central third rail serving as the insulated rail, with pick-up working through brushes situated under the centre of the engines.

By 1939, OO gauge was beginning to make inroads on the O gauge fraternity in Europe, but in America little was done about HO gauge until 1940, and it was not until 1948 that the smaller scale started to become popular there. Then in 1950, Rovex introduced their OO gauge toy trains into England. Unlike the metal models of Hornby-Dublo, these were plastic, and much cheaper than the few Trix-Twin models that were available. They set as a standard the two-rail system, both rails being mounted on a plastic grey base, and thus insulated from each other.

Rovex became Tri-ang, then Tri-ang-Hornby when they subsequently absorbed Hornby-Dublo, but have continued to use the 12 volt DC two-rail system, although they have many times changed the type of track used. At present it is of tinned steel or nickel silver on a plastic base, which represents the wooden cross ties or sleepers.

To keep pace with their rivals, Trix Express, (as Bing was by now known), went over to 12 volts DC operation in 1956, shortly followed by Trix-Twin, both companies using fibre-based track with three insulated rails for the twin system. In 1963 Trix dispensed with their ugly shoes and used the wheels for pick-up, as is now commonplace, and in 1964 they introduced two-rail trackage, which was important in view of a tie-up with Liliput, who made two-rail locos and no three-rail type. By July 1970 Trix Trains had withdrawn all the three-rail Trix-Twin locomotives, and an era had ended.

It was left to Hornby-Dublo to introduce the two-rail system, using nickel silver rail on a plastic moulded base that incorporated the individual sleepers, giving us a track that is now the universal standard. But this was not until 1959, and although their superb locomotives live on under the auspices of Wrenn (who were themselves subsequently acquired by Tri-ang), the Hornby-Dublo trains as such are no more.

The German company Fleischmann was also early in the field with the two-rail system, which they had completely organized by 1956. They now have two parallel systems of trackwork which is some of the best in the world for operating and remote control facilities.

Others, namely the Italian Rivarossi of Como, later joined by Pocher of Turin, and the American company Atlas, started with a three-rail system operating on 15 volts AC, and a two-rail 12 volts DC system. They dropped the three-rail system in the early 1950s, but have developed and refined the two-rail trackwork for their smooth-running rolling stock.

Apart from Atlas, very little progress has been made in the American fields of snap-trackwork. As a result of the influence of the National Model Railroad

Association, a two-rail 12 volts DC system has been standardized, and in addition standards have been drawn up and agreed upon for just about every variable. In Europe, however, there is an astonishing number of different wheel dimensions (and also types of couplers, which will not mix). Thus, because of standardization, the American model railroader has been far ahead of enthusiasts in other countries, since about 1948, when HO gauge became popular. Far ahead, that is, in regard to kits, parts, and the supply of individual items, but not in the field of the toy train or the near-scale model train, for European manufacturers have tended to concentrate their energies on developing the 'train set', to which accessories can be added as and when desired.

Interchange, couplers and wheels

One loner remains: the German firm of Märklin have kept their original style of three-rail operation. Not until 1952 did they introduce their stud-contact system, which they improved in 1970. Although the third rail was taken away with the introduction of the stud-contact system, its place was taken by a series of studs sticking above the ties, contact being made by a shoe or skate under the loco. In addition to this, Märklin operate on an alternating current of up to 15 volts, with a 24 volt reversing circuit. This means that none of the other 16.5 millimetre gauge electric locos can be operated with Märklin equipment.

One other additional power source is overhead wires. There are a number of different catenary sections available for use with pantographs on top of the electric-type locomotives. One advantage of a catenary system is that is is possible to run two locos on one section of the track, one picking up from overhead and using one insulated rail for return current, while the other loco uses the two-rail system in the usual way.

To summarize, therefore: with the exception of Märklin, it should be possible to interchange all model railway rolling stock for 16.5 millimetre gauge. The only

factors that might prevent this are the different types of coupler employed and the dimensions of the wheels, but it is perfectly possible to have one standard coupler on one's own layout. (The Peco type is already found on Trix Train, Trix-Twin, and Hornby-Dublo stock, and can be bought separately. The Tri-ang coupler is neat and unobtrusive, especially if the TT–3 gauge version is purchased for use with the larger trains, being similar to the American LaNal coupler.)

In America the National Model Railroad Association has recommended a contour shape to which all couplers should adhere to be compatible, and to look like the prototype, and in 1971 the German company Fleischmann introduced the 'Fox' coupler, which looks as though it may become a firm favourite with railway modellers. Whatever couplers are used, however, they must of course be mounted properly and at the same height, for otherwise automatic operation, if such is intended, will be impossible.

As for dimensions of wheels, the amount of tolerance available in the different sizes is very little. It is the dimensions of the wheels, combined with the dimensions of trackwork on a turnout, that makes for smooth, difficult, or impossible running.

The dimensions of a model wheel that have to be taken into account are the overall width of the tire, the width, depth and shape of the flange, the width of the tread, and the angle of the tread to the rail. In addition, there is the back-to-back measurement of the two wheels on their axle.

Obviously, if on an ordinary straight piece of track the back-to-back measurement is too wide, then one wheel will ride up on the rail, and if it is too narrow, the wheel will ride in the space between the rails.

The parts of a wheel are shown in the line drawings on page 15, and the different components of the piece of trackwork that is variously known as a point, a switch or a turnout on page 12. There are quite a few different types of point, but we are concerned here only with a straightforward left-hand turnout.

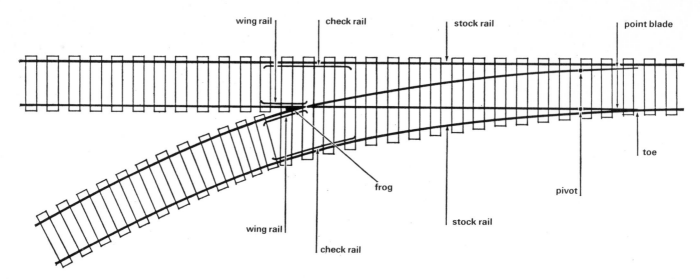

wing rail   check rail   stock rail   point blade

toe

frog   pivot

wing rail

stock rail

check rail

A drawing showing the parts of a point, also known as a turnout or a switch.

Some vital measurements

In order to avoid constant derailments, it is essential that the measurements of the trackwork where two rails cross each other marry with the wheels on your model. The gap between the frog and wing rail must not be too narrow, and must be deep enough to accommodate the flange. The radius of the curved closure rail must not be too sharp, and the check rails must be aligned properly.

If one is using, let us say, Fleischmann trains on Fleischmann track, there is no difficulty; but the use of Tri-ang stock on Hornby-Dublo points may create problems. Fortunately, however, wheels can be changed, and quite a few companies issue excellent scale wheels. One can also purchase scale track, which is often more realistic in operation and to look at than proprietary pieces.

The other 'vital statistics' with which we are concerned are the loading gauge, and the structure gauge. Obviously, a train must not be too high or too wide if it is to enter tunnels, negotiate platforms correctly, or pass other trains. If a model is built to scale, then all bridges, tunnels, and stations must be built to the same scale, and placed in relation to the model as they stood originally in relation to the prototype.

Realism and accuracy are what every modeller tries to strive for, sometimes without appreciating it; but true scale, or at least near-to-scale, models can be the source of an immense amount of satisfaction and pleasure to an enthusiast.

Control and planning

The proprietary manufacturers whose models appear in the colour plates in the second half of this book also make the electrical apparatus that controls the models, but there are also a number of electronic companies, including Codar, and Hammant and Morgan, who make power units specifically for model railways.

Generally speaking, 12 volt motors are used in model locomotives. These incorporate permanent magnets and require direct current. Basically, therefore, a control unit must consist of a transformer to convert the mains current of, for example, 110 volts or 240 volts alternating current into the 12 volts required, a rectifier to convert AC to DC, and a resistance or rheostat to control the amount of power transmitted.

As a result of the great advances in this field, there is no longer any need for bulky equipment, and one can purchase neat packs or units to mount in a control panel, for all the three accepted modern forms of controller. These are the variable voltage or the variable transformer, the earlier resistance controller, and the transistorized controller. Additional devices can be fitted to give extra slow running, various forms of braking or coasting, and remote control or lighting or uncoupling. One may also buy a complete sound pack that will emit any kind of whistle, screech, hiss, puff or clickety-clack noise, through a device in the loco or the tender.

There is no space here to discuss in detail the operation of model railways, the building of scenery, the laying of track upon a baseboard, and the finer forms of control. For information on these subjects the reader is recommended to study some of the many books that are readily available, but in particular to read one or more of the model railway magazines that are issued, generally monthly, in nearly every country of the world. The principal English language publications are two American periodicals, *Model Railroader* and *Railroad Model Craftsman*, and three British magazines, *Model Railways*, *Model Railway Constructor* and *Railway Modeller*. These in turn will lead you to the model railroad hobby shops, where any number of books for further reading and equipment may be purchased.

One of the more important topics discussed among railway modellers is that of layout planning. To start with it is a good idea to settle for one particular country for one's layout, and this choice is not always easy, for there are many types of model available, particularly of American, British, German, French, Scandinavian, Italian, and Swiss trains. Then when this choice has been made, a particular company should be selected, and here once again there is a very wide choice, although not all of the over 430 railroad companies in the USA have their counterpart in proprietary goods! The era may also be chosen, and both old-fashioned locos and the most modern new diesels are easy to come by.

Once country, company, and era are settled, thought should be given to the type of layout to be modelled. This may vary from a vast double mainline track with flyover junctions to a small single branch line in a standard or narrow gauge. The choice is entirely up to the owner, and the choice is wide. Again, lineside accessories for all the kinds of model railways may be bought in various forms, notably metal, castings, plastic and card or wood. The main point is that all these should be kept in proportion, in scale and – of course – in kind.

The types of trains operated should depend entirely on the purpose of the layout; real railways were not laid in an haphazard fashion, but were put down to serve a town or a port or an industry. Once one has decided upon the locale of the miniature railway train, formations can be made up to serve the points of interest, and thus locos and stock can be bought or made or assembled which will fit the scene like a glove. A layout will be more effective if it is inspired by a single idea, and if it is then carried through, right down to the choice of the smallest accessories.

Passenger and freight units

Many of the models illustrated in the pages that follow can be purchased in North America or Britain today, and can be used to form different kinds of train formations. The following are some possible units:

Express: For model expresses it is usual to have six or seven coaches hauled by powerful steam locos, of the Pacific Class or larger, or one or more diesels. Rolling stock can include dining cars, passenger cars, and perhaps vista-dome or observation cars. If you prefer large steam locos and have not much space, it is as well to remember that many 4–6–2 locos ended their journeys on long hauls pulling only a couple of coaches, having dropped or slipped others en route.

Night expresses: Four or five sleeping cars, hauled by a large loco or diesel unit, are the most usual. There are excellent models of both British and Continental Wagons-Lits on the market.

Main-line trains: Space decrees that fifteen-coach trains are difficult; the odd thing is that in miniature they do not look real. Four or five cars with, perhaps, a buffet car and certainly a baggage car or a brake-composite make a good combination. Multiple unit electric trains or diesel units are quite commonly used for these trains.

Suburban traffic: This varies from country to country and from era to era. One can use a 2–6–4T tank engine and a couple of suburban non-corridor coaches, or a twin-unit diesel set, or an electric set, or electric locos with overhead pantographs pulling a few cars.

Local traffic: Again, many variations are feasible. Small tank locos, or a diesel railcar, or interurban units or trolley cars, or push-pull cars with a loco between are all commonly used.

Branch lines: Enthusiasts of early models often want to use four or six-wheel coaches hauled by baby tank locos, whereas others prefer to use the more up-to-date diesel railcar. Where only a small space is available, a branch line model is suggested.

Milk trains: Various types of milk tankers are in use, and four or five of these with a utility van and a brake van, and sometimes also a passenger car form a suitable unit.

Breakdown: A 'Big Hook' with its attendant flat cars and a

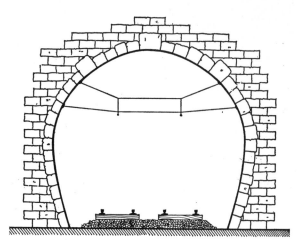

Right: Two diagrams showing typical contours for double track and single track tunnels, one containing overhead traction pickup wires.

brake van each end are necessary here, although a smaller version could make use of a crane truck. Track-laying trains also use the same set, and should include long flat cars to carry the rails.

Mail-trains: A Travelling Post Office car, with or without automatic pick-up apparatus is common, and several parcels cars can be incorporated as required. Note that 'Ocean Mails' cars are not used on mail trains, but on boat trains.

Boat trains: These generally consist of first class passenger cars and a couple of Pullman cars. Utility vans or 'Ocean Mails' cars make up this rake.

Pullman trains: Various countries run Pullmans in different colours. The different types of car can be made up into a rake of five or six; remember, however, that these cars are normally heavier than passenger coaches and a large loco unit may well be needed.

Additions: Many vacuum-brake fitted vehicles are run with passenger trains; these may include one or more milk tank wagons, parcels vans, baggage cars, utility vans, perishable fish or fruit vans, theatre scenery cars, and furniture container assemblies. It is up to the individual, of course, to select the additional pieces that he needs.

So far we have only mentioned varieties of passenger trains. Freight trains, too, are many and varied, but in each case they should consist of wagons or cars that serve the needs of the layout. Thus, food, in meat and fish vans or in vegetable and milk wagons, together with general goods in parcels or utility vans, can be carried to all inhabited areas. Again, coal is an essential freight commodity and is taken in open wagons or in hopper cars to serve towns or loco sheds, power stations or lineside industries. All other cars serve special purposes; for example, salt wagons at salt works, ore cars at mines, fish vans at ports, and wine containers at vineyards.

Model classification

In the captions that follow, the Whyte classification of wheel arrangements is used, since it is more commonly used, both in the USA and in Britain for the description of steam locomotives. With this system of classification, the first figure indicates the number of pilot wheels, the second figure the driving wheels and the third figure the trailing wheels. On the Continent of Europe the number of axles is counted, so that a 4–6–2 would be a 2–C–1, the driving wheels being represented by the appropriate letter of the alphabet. The suffix T indicates a tank loco.

Diesel-Electric, Diesel-Mechanical, Electric and Gas-Turbine locos are classified differently, and here a number is allotted to each non-powered wheel and a letter for each powered wheel, as they are seen from one side. The suffix letter 'o' is added after the main letter to indicate a double-powered bogie (or truck), and if two bogies (powered or double-powered) are coupled by a drive shaft, a plus sign (+) is included in the classification. Let us take an example for explanation. Plate 49 shows a loco whose wheels would be described by Whyte as a 4–4–4–4, but in electric loco parlance as 2 – Bo + Bo – 2, indicating two non-powered two wheel bogies fore and aft, and two double-powered bogies in the centre, connected by a drive shaft.

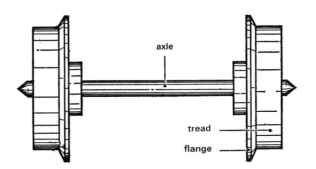

The most important dimensions of a model wheel are the overall width of the tire, the width, depth and shape of the flange, the width of the tread, the angle of the tread to the rail, and the back-to-back measurement of the two wheels on their axle.

Locomotives that bear certain types of wheel arrangements have been given specific names, eg:

2-4-2	Columbia	2-4-4	Hungary
2-6-0	Mogul	2-6-2	Prairie
2-6-4	Adriatic	2-6-6-6	Allegheny
2-8-0	Consolidation	2-8-2	Mikado
2-8-4	Berkshire	2-10-2	Santa Fe
2-10-4	Texas	2-12-4	Bulgaria
4-4-0	American	4-4-2	Atlantic
4-4-4	Dominion	4-6-2	Pacific
4-6-4	Hudson	4-6-6-4	Challenger
4-8-2	Mountain	4-8-4	Northern
4-8-8-4	Big Boy	4-10-0	Mastodon
4-10-2	Overland	4-14-4	Andriev

Finally, the types and styles of passenger cars and the liveries in use are faithfully reproduced in the shape and colourings used in the models illustrated. In Britain drab blue and grey have replaced the four distinct colourings common before 1948, but even these last could not compete with the tones, tints, shades and linings used by over 120 different railway companies before 1923, when they were grouped into the four major companies that lasted for the next quarter of a century.

Model railways is one of the world's most popular hobbies, claimed by some to be the biggest of all. Perhaps this book can help to show the newcomer some of the fascination which absorbs so many people in so many different countries.

Bibliography

Ahern, J. H., *Miniature landscape modelling*, Model & Allied Publishers (England)

Andress, M., *Narrow gauge model railways*, Almark (England)

Beal, E., *Railway modelling in miniature*, Model & Allied Publishers (England)

Carter, E. F., *The model railway encyclopedia*, Harold Starke (England)

Freezer, C. J., *A home for your railway*, Peco Publications (England)

Freezer, C. J., *Railway modeller shows you how booklets (20)*, Peco Publications (England)

Hertz, L. H., *The complete book of model railroading*, Simmons-Boardman (USA)

McClanahan, W., *Scenery for model railroads*, Kalmbach (USA)

Roche, F. J., and Templer, G. G., *Building model locomotives*, Ian Allen (England)

Simmons, N., *How to go railway modelling*, Patrick Stephens (England)

Sutton, D., *The complete book of model railroading*, Prentice Hall (USA)

Warren, R., *764 helpful hints for model railroaders*, Kalmbach (USA)

Westcott, L. H., *How to wire your model railroad*, Kalmbach (USA)

1–2 The early railways are not quite as well represented in model form as perhaps they should be, but this is one example. The Trix Express replica of 'Der Adler' is slightly larger than the normal Continental scale of 3.5 mm to the foot because it would have been too small otherwise. The locomotive is not mechanized, but is run by an electric motor in the second coach (the pick-up can be seen in front of the wheel).

The original 'Adler' opened the first German rail link between Fürth and Nuremberg in 1835, and a hundred years later it was rebuilt. In 1960 it was put back into service before being consigned to the Nuremberg transport museum.

This model shows the early type of passenger car, which consisted of one or more mail-coach bodies of the sort drawn by horses.

1

2

3
4

3–4 The 'General' not only featured in a famous Buster Keaton film, but was part of an actual event during the American Civil War, during which it changed hands several times.

The Mantua Tyco model of this 4–4–0 American-type locomotive features a 12 volt motor in the tender which drives the four main wheels via a rubber-shaft, visible in the photograph. The other locomotive which took part in the Keaton chase, the 'Texas', is also the subject of an HO Gauge model, as are a number of other American locomotives of the same era.

5   6

5   The superstructure of model locomotives is generally made of tin, a lead-tin alloy (often called 'white metal'), plastic compounds, or of copper sheet or brass as shown here. Different techniques of painting have to be used on these various surfaces. Many Japanese-built models of American locomotives, like the Tenshodo 0–4–0T Switcher shown here, are available in unpainted form.

6   A tank locomotive is one in which the supply of water is carried not in a separate tender but in tanks, which are described as pannier, saddle, or side. Shown is one of the four American tank locos, a Tenshodo 0–6–0T of a Baldwin Locomotive Works prototype.

7   Reclassified by the German Federal System as Class 89, several Class T3 0–6–0T tank locos of the old Prussian State Railways were still in service in 1963. The Fleischmann HO model has two operating headlights.

7

8 One of the older types of side-tank engines still in use with the Italian State Railways is the 0–6–0T Gr.835 loco used for shunting. This Rivarossi model is alongside one of the many different types of water-crane, this one modelled by Pocher.

9 The 0–6–0T Class 89 tank engine of the German Federal Railways appeared in 1927, and various versions with different sizes of side tanks were produced. An early version is shown in this Märklin model.

10 In 1922 the Italian State Railways Gr.940 type of tank loco was introduced for light passenger and freight service, and some are still serving in mountain regions of Italy. Only a few tank engines had the 2–8–2T ('Mikado') arrangement seen in this Rivarossi model.

11 The Tenshodo model of a 2–6–4T tank loco used mainly on iron ore trains of the Statens Järnvägar (Swedish State Railways) has a smart black livery and shows a certain amount of British influence.

12 13

12 Over 150 engines of the British Railways 4–MT (Power Classification 4–Mixed Traffic) 2–6–4T locomotives were built from 1948 onwards. They were developed from the London, Midland and Scottish Railway Stanier engines which were themselves originally taken from a large suburban passenger tank introduced by Sir Henry Fowler in 1927. The Hornby-Dublo model depicts this successful and extensive class of heavy tank.

13 A head-on-view of the Japanese-built model of the Swedish tank loco shown in Plate 11. Some fine detail can be observed, including the 'jewels' used as headlights.

14–15–16 The Altini model shown in these three pictures is of a steam engine with an unconventional form of motive power – a multi-cylinder steam locomotive with direct drive. The large inclined cylinders and the positions of the cranks can be clearly seen. The most modern locomotive of this kind was the (British) Southern Railway 'Leader' Class of 1948.

16

17 One of the most popular American models on model railroads is the diminutive switching engine. This example is the Rivarossi version of the Class C–16a of the Baltimore and Ohio railroad.

18 The 0–6–0 tender locomotives on American railroads were used for switching or for hauling light freight trains. This Altini model has a funnel used on wood-burning locos.

19

19 One of the smaller American railroads with only eighty route miles was the Maryland & Pennsylvania. This is a brass United model by Tenshodo of a 2–8–0 Consolidation used on short-run branch-line freight services in 1912.

20 In 1900 the famous Schenectady Locomotive Works built their 4–4–2 Atlantic, of which this is a collector's model, for the large Chicago and North Western Railway.

21 The 4–6–2 Pacific locomotive was one of the largest classes of locomotive built in the world, primarily for fast passenger trains. The American example modelled here was developed from the large-wheeled Atlantic depicted above.

20

21

22

23

22 The 2–8–2 Mikado, of which this is a Tenshodo model, was built in various versions including this heavy Class 0–8 (367,000 lbs), of which twenty-five operated on the Great Northern from 1932.

23 In 1929 the Baldwin Locomotive Works built six Class S–1 4–8–4 Northern locos for the Great Northern Railway Company which also featured a twelve-wheel Vanderbilt tender like that shown in Plate 22. This, too, is a Tenshodo model of a fast freight and passenger loco.

24–25–26 Two hundred and sixty 4–6–4 Hudson locomotives were built for the New York Central System. The Class J-3 was the final phase of this fine type, which replaced the 4–6–2 Pacific locos from 1927 onwards and which were themselves replaced by the 4–8–4 Northerns. (In Europe the 4–6–4 wheel arrangement is referred to as 'Baltic'.) The three views are of a Tenshodo model of a 1937 prototype.

26

27

28

27–28 The largest driving wheels used on a prototype engine of this type were the 74-inch diameter shown on the Tenshodo model of a 2–10–4 Texas type built in 1944 by Baldwin for the Atchison, Topeka & Santa Fe Railroad. This freight engine was derived from the earlier 2–10–2 Santa Fe type.

29 The Japanese firm of Tenshodo have made models of more than a hundred American locomotives; this is the front view of one of the large ones.

30 Among the larger compound Mallet articulated locos there are those with the following wheel arrangements: 2–8–8–0, 2–8–8–2, 2–8–8–4, 4–8–8–2 and 4–8–8–4 Big Boy. The Tenshodo model is of a 2–8–8–4 Class EM-1 of which the Baltimore and Ohio Railroad had thirty in service on coal trains in West Virginia in 1944. In a Mallet locomotive, both engines are placed under the boiler and the front one is on a separate bogie truck pivoted under the fore-part.

31 The Castle Class was one of the more successful locomotives built for a railway, in this case the Great Western, which first appeared in 1924. This is a Hornby-Dublo model in early British Railways livery.

32 The A–4 Pacific was designed for high-speed passenger service between London and Newcastle for the London and North Eastern Railway. 'Mallard' of this class achieved 126 mph in 1938. Hornby-Dublo issued this garter-blue liveried version of the locomotive named after the A–4 designer.

33 Fleischmann have produced this model of a Class 41 2–8–2 of the German Federal Railways, complete with three headlights and smoke-deflectors. The prototype was used on long hauls for freight and occasionally for passenger trains in hilly regions.

34 The Prussian State Railways used a 4–6–0 Class 38 for mixed passenger and freight services. This Liliput model has a Seuthe smoke unit concealed in the boiler.

35

35 This is a Rivarossi model of a 2–8–0 freight locomotive, known as a type Gr.740, of the Italian State Railways. It is in the typical livery of black superstructure and red running plate, solebar and wheels.

36 The Gr.691 of the Italian State Railways was one of the more powerful of their steam locomotives. This is a Rivarossi model of the 4–6–2 Pacific which, until 1956, was still to be seen on main lines throughout Italy.

36

37

37 The Illinois Terminal Railroad is a freight line, most of which has been electrified for some time. An overhead 600 volt system is used, and a model made by Suydam of one of the early C Class B+B+B+B locos is shown here, complete with two trolley poles.

38 Featuring a single pantograph with twin collectors, this is a Lionel model of a Co-Co locomotive of 3,300 hp for 11,000 volts single-phase, 25-cycle AC used by the Virginian Railway Company, but here shown in the livery of the New York, New Haven & Hartford Railroad.

38

39 Märklin make this model of an electric shunting loco. It is a C Class E63 of the German Federal Railways with a gear-driven jackshaft.

40 The Bo+Bo German Federal Railways Class E44 was a general purpose electric locomotive for either suburban passenger or mixed freight trains. This model was made by Märklin.

41 A number of model manufacturers duplicate products. In this plate are the Trix Express (German) and Liliput (Austrian) versions of the Co+Co E94 electric goods locomotive which was the heaviest of its kind in 1940 when it went into service with the German Federal Railways, weighing 122 tons.

2

42 The Bo+Bo Class E40 of the German Federal Railways is in green (freight) livery. The prototype of the Fleischmann model weighs 185,136 lbs. The Class E10 passenger express loco is almost identical, and appears in several other liveries including blue, blue and ivory, and red and ivory.

43 The Class Ce 6/8 of the Swiss Federal Railway is an articulated 1–Co+Co–1 electric loco, nick-named the 'Crocodile' because of its appearance as it slides around the curves of the St Gotthard line. Märklin make this example of a heavy freight locomotive.

3

44

45
46

44 Forty-three multipurpose Class BB 12000 locos of the Bo-Bo wheel arrangement were built for the Paris–Lille line of the French National Railways. It weighs $76\frac{1}{2}$ tons and in the blue livery shown hauls mineral wagons in eastern France on the Valenciennes–Thionville route. Fleischmann made this model.

45–46 Two views of the Pocher model of the Co-Co CC7101 locomotive are shown here. This type hauls express passenger trains on the Paris–Lyons line of the French National Railways at an average speed of 77 mph. Built by Alsthom, these locos have reached speeds of over 200 mph on several occasions since 1955.

47 Originally appearing in 1928 for use in southern Italy on heavy freight trains, the Gr.E626 of the Italian State Railways is in two halves, being articulated. This Bo + Bo + Bo loco, of which a Rivarossi model is shown, was followed by the similar E636 built in both freight and passenger versions, with differing transmission ratios.

48 The Class E424 Bo + Bo modelled here by Märklin appeared in 1943 and is commonly used all over Italy on light freight or light passenger duties.

49

50

51

49–50 There have been three series of the Italian State Railways Class E428 2–Bo + Bo–2 loco. Rivarossi make models of all three. Both the model in Plate 49 and the Fleischmann version in Plate 50 are of the Series II, with an articulated underframe. The prototype has eight electric motors. The three series may be identified by the progressive improvement in the streamlining.

51 In 1959 the Class E646 Bo + Bo + Bo appeared on the Italian State Railways. Rivarossi built this model featuring the articulated arrangement visible here. It was used on the heavier passenger and freight trains.

52 Rivarossi also model the second series of the Class E646 of the Italian State Railways which has a different shape of cab (at each end) from the earlier engines. It is probably the most powerful of present-day Italian electric locomotives.

52

53 The Baldwin-Westinghouse Model S-12 1200 hp switching locomotive was bought by over seventy railroads in the USA. Fleischmann used to make the B-B model shown here in two of the many liveries employed.

54 Tenshodo models of the Electro-Motive Division of General Motors Corporation's GP–9 (general purpose) and SD–9 (special duty hood unit). These B–B and C–C locos are road switchers for operating in yards. They spelt the end of the American steam loco by reason of their superior operational ability.

55 Tenshodo and Rivarossi models of the EMD–General Motors B–B Model F–7 of 1500 hp are shown below. Designed for heavy duty passenger service as well as for their primary function as pullers of freight, these locos are available in A (with a cab) or B units. These may be coupled A–A, A–B, A–B–B, A–B–B–A, or A–B–A, to give up to 6,000 hp. Over sixty US railroads use these locomotives.

56 The Krupp works in Essen builds the Class V60 diesel switcher, which is classified C and has a blind-shaft drive. Of 650 hp, this German Federal Railways loco is used in yards. The model is by Fleischmann.

57 Of the classic shape to be seen on several European railways, Märklin's model of the German Federal Railways Class V200 Bo + Bo diesel is similar in outline to the British Rail type 4 B–B 'Warship' Class of 2,200 brake horse-power.

58

59

58 In 1953 British Railways introduced an 0–6–0 diesel shunter. Over a thousand were built of Classes 08, 09 and in 1955, ten of this ubiquitous 350 bhp locomotive, of which Hornby-Dublo made the model here.

59 Over twenty Class 55 'Deltic' locos have been put into service by British Railways (later British Rail) since 1961, each powered by two Napier Deltic engines of 1,650 bhp. The Co-Co here is by Hornby-Dublo.

60 Used on secondary lines for passenger and freight services is the Class D342 of the Italian State Railways. This diesel locomotive model is made by Lima.

61 Diesel railcars of the German type shown here are normally used in single or twin units (one motor car and one trailer) on local suburban services. This is a Fleischmann model.

62 The Fiat 7145B made for the Italian State Railways is available in two colour schemes from Rivarossi. The prototype motor coach ALn 668 may have a trailer.

63 Electric railcars also exist in some countries and the Altini model of a twin-articulated unit using three trucks is similar to other European motor coaches.

60

61

62

63

64 Many old passenger coaches had a clerestory (clear story) – a row of long windows raised above the roof line – for ventilation, as is seen in this Pocher model of a Swedish State Railways Type C third class coach.

65 Fleischmann modelled this second and third class coach, Class BCi Pr 98a of the former Prussian State Railways. This was an 1878 coach.

66 In the background is a Fleischmann model of a baggage and mail car, class Pw Posti Pr 92 of the Prussian State Railways, and in front of it is a Märklin model of a six-wheeled (later Class C3) Prussian compartment coach. The prototype was dull grey and there were four classes of travel, of which the fourth was very primitive.

67

68

67 The green coach on the left is a Fleischmann model of a Class Bymb second class coach of the German Federal Railway. On the right is a Rivarossi model of a Class Bz second class coach of the Italian State Railways.

68 Comparison between two different scales is shown in this photograph of a Fleischmann HO Gauge model which is $9\frac{5}{8}$ inches in length overall, and a 6½ inch long N Gauge model by Arnold-Rapido, both of a Trans-Europ Express car, Class AV4um. (Both cars are first class, the former with compartments and the latter with a centre aisle.)

69 The chocolate and cream livery of the early Western Region, contrasting
with the plum colour of the Midland Region coaches in the 1950s shows in
this photograph of Hornby-Dublo tinplate models of British Railways
passenger rolling stock.

70 In front is a HOrnby-acHO model of a second class French National
Railways coach. This is an older type of vehicle.

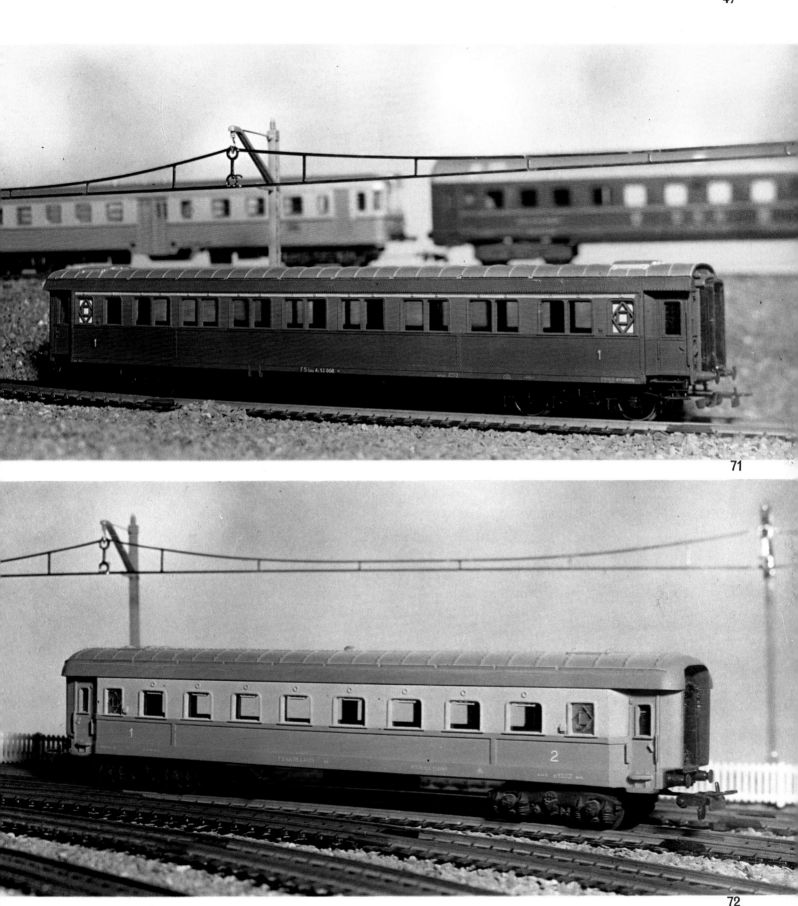

71

72

71 This is a Rivarossi model of a first class coach of the Italian State Railways, type Az 52000. The Bz 31000 second class car is similar, but has a centre aisle and not compartments.

72 Pocher also makes models of the Az 52000 first class and Bz 31000 second class coaches of the Italian State Railways in the dark and bright blue livery used experimentally in the fifties, as well as in brown and fawn (see Plate 71).

73 Fleischmann made these models of a passenger coach and a baggage-coach combine in the livery of the New York, New Haven & Hartford Railroad.

74 These are Athearn models of 'standard coaches', a dining car and a baggage-mail combine of the Atchison, Topeka & Santa Fe Railroad.

75 Streamlined cars followed the 'standard coaches', and Tenshodo modelled a streamlined observation car shown here with an observation dome. This also appeared on the Santa Fe Railroad.

76 The International Sleeping Car Company has blue and white Pullman cars, blue restaurant cars, and blue baggage cars. These are Pocher models.

77 Liliput make models of earlier cars used by the international companies on European expresses. The blue one is a Pullman, and the teak coloured coach is a dining car of the Swiss Federal Railways on the St Gotthard Line.

78

79

80

78 The International Sleeping Car Company has introduced modern equipment in recent years. The model by Pocher is of a sleeping-car made by Fiat, type 15G no 4581.

79 The German Sleeping Car and Dining Car Company (DSG) uses sleeping cars like this Pocher model of a class WLAB4um. Both first class and second class versions exist.

80 In front is a Märklin model of a German Federal Railways goods traffic luggage van, type Pwg. Behind is a Pocher model of a Swiss Federal Railways Class Fz4ü baggage and post van.

81 This is the famous Armistice Coach. An old dining car of the International Sleeping Car Company, No. 2419 was used both in 1918 and in 1940 for the signing of Armistices between France and Germany. It no longer exists. The Germans blew up the museum in which it was housed near Compiègne in 1940, and destroyed the car itself in 1945 at Ohrdruf. The Pocher model shown here is complete with all the interior fittings of the original teak vehicle.

82 An unusual model, by Pocher, is of the car used by President Lincoln on his train trips in the USA. It has four bogies or trucks for smooth riding and to support the weight of the fittings.

83

84

85

83 This is a Rivarossi model of a goods van type F1925 of the Italian State Railways. Similar four-wheeled vans are used all over Europe.

84 Märklin make this model of a Swiss Federal Railways Type SBB-K3 box car, with a cabin for the brakeman at one end.

85 The German Federal Railways uses this four-wheeled box car. It has two sliding doors. This is a Fleischmann model of a Type Gimmehs 57 vehicle.

86

86 HOrnby-acHO issues this model of a refrigerator van used by the STEF Company in France.

87 There are four types of British brake van: the closed van, the vestibule type, the verandah, and the platform. All Great Western Railway vans were of exactly the same pattern, the single verandah type. This Hornby-Dublo model is typical of the 16 ton version.

88 The type Poz 1920 flat car of the Italian State Railways is often used for carrying rails. The stakes are removable. There is also a version with a brakeman's cabin at one end, and models of each are made by Rivarossi. The Italian style of loading gauge in this photograph is made by Pocher.

87

88

89   In the foreground are two type Poz 1920 flat cars (seen in the previous plate) used together with military models by Lesney and Micromodels. The 2–8–2T tank loco is a model by Rivarossi of the Italian State Railways Class 940. The coach is by Lima.

90   The Red Cross or hospital train is made up of some of the early Lima models of cars and vans.

91   These models of Italian wagons are by various manufacturers. The attractive crane wagon is by Pocher. Other models are by Electrotren, Lima and Rivarossi.

92   Tram locomotives have appeared in various countries. This Lima model is typical of the narrow gauge trains used on local lines in Europe, hauling two or three small passenger cars. The track gauge of this model is 9 mm.

93   This is a tram, trolley-car or interurban, made by Tenshodo. With their standard gauge of 4 feet 8½ inches, trams were used a great deal in metropolitan cities until ousted by the diesel-engined omnibus. Pickup was from overhead wire or via a carrier running in a slot in a centre rail.

93

94 In Germany many trams hauled single-deck trailers. This is a Hamo model.

95 In Milan earlier this century, tramcars of the Edison type were used, sometimes pulling a trailer car. This is a Rivarossi model, for which special road sections with inset rail are available.

96 Among the many models of figures available in various scales are those of Merit and Prieser (shown here), and Merten, Airfix and Peco.

97 Each of these points, turnouts or switches is for remote control, and contains solenoids which operate spring-loaded closure rails. The Märklin points with stud contacts are shown on the left, the first being scale model track and the other standard track. Next is a Fleischmann point which has four spring clips. Wires attached to different clips and various accessories enable various forms of automatic operation. On the right is a Trix Express point with a centre third rail, actually the common return, as each of the outer rails is used for independent pickups.

97

100

101

98 Fleischmann makes this particular model of the 90-ton German Type 6700 Nür crane. The complete model consists of the crane-car tender to support the boom in transit, the idler car carrying wood blocks (at the back on the right), the crane car itself, and the counterweight car; the weights are missing in this photograph.

99 Just about every type of bridge is available for model railway enthusiasts. This is a single span girder bridge, but there are short-arch girders with bows above or below, long box-girder bridges, viaducts, timber trestle bridges, and so on.

100 Tunnel mouths, like this Faller model, of various kinds, compositions and shapes are also obtainable. (The VT 45 railcar in the livery of the Austrian Federal Railways, is a Lima model.)

101 Scenery adds to the realism of a model. The buildings are by Kibri, the trees by Britains and Faller, the figures by Merit, and the rocks are natural.

102

103

104

102–103 Two more views of the scene shown in Plate 101 give an overall impression of an Alpine railway station.

104 This freight station has Märklin track, Vollmer buildings, HOrnby acHO signals, a Rivarossi loco, and wagons by various makers.

105 The Märklin goods van is being loaded with Merit freight.

106 An unusual scene is this Pocher closed goods wagon being conveyed on a road trailer.

105

106

107

108

109

110

107 This is a model of a Continental railway station, a continuation of which can be seen in the next photograph.

108 Models by various manufacturers have been used to compose this station scene, of which a third view is in the next plate.

109 The number of model trains in the station gives an air of activity to the picture.

110 On the right foreground is a transformer. There are controllers on both sides of the panel. The Märklin switch panels in blue cases are for switching on or off the train and lighting circuits; the two with green buttons on the right operate points and signals. The eleven distributor panels for the sections are in the centre.

111–112 By day or by night, with or without model people, a model railway station holds the attention of the spectator.

111-112